DANCING IN THE ELEVATOR

A Compilation of Anecdotes
about Life
with Alzheimer Disease

D0809535

Dancing
in the Elevator

A Compilation of Anecdotes
about Life
with Alzheimer Disease

Barbara Schulman
Beverly Grostern
Donna Lordon

ISBN: 0-9739963-0-7

Published by BB&D
(Barbara Schulman, Beverly Grostern
and Donna Lordon)

Printed and bound in Ottawa, Ontario,
Canada by Gilmore Printing Services

Cover design by Ilana Grostern

SPONSORS

The authors are grateful to the following sponsors:

$1000
Central Park Lodges Ottawa

Kelly Funeral Homes

National Bank Financial Ltd.

UNDER $1000
Retire-at-Home Services Inc.

Pathways to Memory by Homewatch CareGivers

IN-KIND CONTRIBUTIONS
Gilmore Printing Services

May Court Club of Ottawa

Prosebusters Communications

Contents

Acknowledgements

Whille producing the book has given us some serious moments, it has also brought a great deal of pleasure, joy, and learning. We never anticipated how enriching this experience would be or that our friendship, already strong, would grow even stronger in the process.

We are grateful to many friends for helping to make this book a reality and for their unconditional support. We would like to express our warmest thanks to Miriam Bloom and Donna Bates for providing guidance and expertise with layout, design, and typesetting. We would also like to thank Ilana Grostern who designed the book cover and helped with graphics. Thank you to Fay Rogers for her useful feedback on content. Finally, many thanks to Kathy Wright and the staff of the Alzheimer Society of Ottawa for their belief in and active support for this book.

Why this book?

As my mother's memory gradually deteriorated, I took heart in the lighter moments we shared together. So as not to forget these special times, I began to jot them down in a diary. When the going got tough, which it did from time to time, I would look back on my notes and these anecdotes would inevitably bring a smile to my face. They are moments I will treasure forever.

About two years ago, I had the idea of compiling a book of such anecdotes. I thought that sharing these brighter moments might provide comfort and inspiration to others with family and friends with Alzheimer Disease, who know only too well how long and difficult the journey can be.

I explored my idea with the Alzheimer Society of Ottawa and with some others in the community. I was pleasantly overwhelmed by the positive response I received both from professionals working in the field and from those whose lives have been touched by dementia.

I then decided to pursue the initiative. I asked two longtime friends, Beverly Grostern and Donna

Lordon, to join me in writing this book. Without much coercion on my part, we began in earnest to make this dream a reality. We subsequently embarked on a partnership with the Alzheimer Society of Ottawa and made plans to write the book and launch it at the Society's 2006 annual meeting with all proceeds going to the Society.

The book contains contributions from eleven caregivers, mostly family and friends of people with Alzheimer Disease in the Ottawa community. Though we sometimes made some minor changes to the stories, we have made every effort to retain their authenticity. Everyone associated with the book acknowledged the value that a light approach could bring to those whose loved ones suffer from dementia. Perhaps some of these stories may even be of assistance to caregivers.

There are countless heartwrenching stories of caring for people with Alzheimer Disease. In no way is this book intended to diminish the incredibly difficult struggles caregivers often face.

It is very challenging to try to understand the thoughts and actions of persons with Alzheimer Disease. Sometimes just as we think we understand their behaviour, we discover that our insights are incorrect. Yet at other times, our rationale appears to be perfect. We may be able to explain certain patterns and yet find it frustrating that other patterns are inexplicable.

By sharing our experiences – both the good and the bad – we believe that family, friends, caregivers and, ultimately, people with Alzheimer Disease will benefit. Hopefully this book will be one venue for such sharing to occur.

Barbara Schulman

WITH STORY CONTRIBUTIONS FROM:
Joan Costello
Christine Davis
Madeleine Honeyman
Donna Lordon
Irene McCullough
Della Nordick
Victor Rabinovitch
Barbara Schulman
Kathy Wright, and
Two anonymous contributors

NOTE TO THE READER:
The names of some of the individuals in this book have been changed to protect their privacy or the privacy of their families.

The personalities of our loved ones

Even as Alzheimer Disease encroaches upon them, our beloved family and friends can still surprise, inspire, delight, and comfort us with their retention of familiar character and the emergence of aspects hitherto unknown to us, their efforts to adapt to their deficits, the tenacity of their early learning and habits, and their enjoyment of the moment.

STILL THEMSELVES

THE THEME OF THIS FIRST AND LARGEST group of anecdotes is how persons with Alzheimer Disease display long-familiar character traits, sometimes in surprising ways and at unexpected times!

Dancing in the elevator

I will never forget the day I took my mother to several related medical appointments and experienced one frustration after another in doing so (for example, we had parking difficulties, then my mother did not fully comprehend why we needed to attend these medical appointments and continually asked if we could go home, we waited at every appointment for my mother to be seen, and my mother again suggested that we just go home because it was a waste of time!). When we finally returned to her apartment building and were in the elevator going to her floor, my mother spontaneously began to sing one of her familiar tunes and started dancing in the elevator. She was as content as content could be and totally oblivious to the hectic and terrible day we had experienced.

Watering flowers: a whole new approach

I was doing my regular check of my mother's apartment to make sure all was well. I would routinely inspect her plants, as my mother has a tendency to overwater them and the water could often be found overflowing or dripping onto a tablecloth, the floor or a table. On this particular occasion, I was doing some light dusting and came across her crystal vase filled with silk flowers. It quickly became obvious that my mother had also begun to water the silk flowers. I gently mentioned to her that silk flowers did not need to be watered and suggested that I empty the water from the vase. My mother was quick to reply that I should leave everything as is – the water can't hurt the flowers!

A different grapevine…

My mother was always fastidious about keeping her fruit in the fridge. One day I was cleaning up the contents of her refrigerator and came across a very robust bunch of grapes. Upon closer examination I discovered that the grapes were plastic. I immediately checked my mother's fruit bowl where there was an assortment of plastic fruit including plastic grapes – thinking that maybe my mother had inadvertently put them in the fridge. However, the grapes were in the fruit bowl where they belonged. So whence came the plastic grapes in the fridge? Did my mother buy the grapes at the local supermarket? Did the cashier realize this? Did the cashier weigh the grapes?

Enduring love

My favourite memory of my sister is of sitting on the lawn with her and looking at her family photograph album. She always said, "That's the little one and that's the big one," as she could no longer remember names. I would turn the page to a picture of her husband and she would turn the page and I would turn it back and say, "Who is this?" She would turn the page, I would pretend to be angry and say, "Don't you know his name? Tell me." She would get a secret smile on her face and put her hand over her heart and say, "I keep him in here."

Back to the future

Like many of us, my mother would always prepare a list of things to buy when we went grocery shopping. Inevitably, over the past several years she had been increasingly inclined to misplace these lists. She had a habit of writing her grocery lists on the back of old grocery bills. I recall one occasion when we were grocery shopping and my mother enlisted my assistance in rummaging through her purse to find her grocery list. Well, yes, we did succeed in finding it. What amused me most was that the grocery list was on the back of a grocery bill dated 1999. We were then in 2003!

A special thank you

As soon as my mother showed frequent lapses in memory, her family physician agreed to refer her to the memory clinic at the hospital. After the initial assessment and diagnosis, my mother began regular visits (approximately twice a year) to the memory clinic, where she was fortunate to have a very fine, kind and competent physician. I often sat in on the regular testing that the physician would conduct to determine the extent of deterioration since the previous visit.

For the last part of the assessment, my mother's physician would ask her to write a sentence. By this stage in the progression of the disease, I wondered if my mother would even be able to write a sentence. Well, she most certainly did remember how to do so. The sentence she formulated and which was obviously written with her doctor in mind was, "Thank you for helping me." Invariably at each routine six-month visit, she composed the same sentence.

Mind your own business

On every visit to my mother's apartment I would try to check the status of the food in my mother's refrigerator. Did she have fresh vegetables and fruit? Had anything gone bad? Had certain items (especially yogurt and other dairy products) overextended their shelf life? And so on.

It was not unusual for me to throw out a few items and stock up on others. This I had to try to do in snippets of time when my mother was in the washroom or otherwise preoccupied, as one of the few things she seriously objected to was anyone going through her fridge. A friend whose mother had Alzheimer Disease gave me a wonderful tip that would at least make my fridge forays less excruciating. She told me to avoid consulting with my mother on whether something should be thrown out; if I thought it should be thrown out, "Just do it."

On this particular occasion when I was checking my mother's fridge and was just about to throw out some items, my mother caught me in the act. She insisted that I put the items back in the fridge where they had been and told me to take care of my own fridge instead!

Coats galore

My sister Dorothy loved the day program she attended and used to gather her coats – *all* her coats – on the chesterfield each day in readiness. One day I went to tell her a visitor was coming, that we should put the coats away and that I would help her. She glared at me and said, "I can do it myself." Collecting the coats she started up the stairs. Over her shoulder she pointed at me and in a disgusted voice said, "School teacher!"

Some habits die hard...

My mother was quite observant of certain Jewish traditions including that of lighting Sabbath candles every Friday evening. As her disease progressed, her formal caregivers and I became increasingly concerned that she was still lighting her candles each week, potentially placing herself and the others in her building at risk. To be fair, she was mindful of the danger and frequently told me that she never left the apartment while the candles were lit. I tried to convince her to use an electric version of candlesticks but I was not the least bit surprised that she would have nothing to do with that idea.

I thought that perhaps with time, lighting the candles would be forgotten like so many other habits had been. But no such luck. She continued to light her candles every Friday evening with very few exceptions and very little supervision. Her ritual continues in her group residence where she and many others still light candles. Fortunately now she is in a safe and secure environment in which to do so!

Expertise valued

My sister was an expert needlewoman and took pleasure in it. She was proud that she was the only one who could turn up trousers using a feather stitch and that the staff at the day program she attended brought her their skirts and pants to be tailored.

Shopping revisited

As my mother became less comfortable traveling within the city, she established a routine whereby she walked or took the bus to the local shopping centre (within nine blocks of her apartment) probably six days a week.

In the evening when I called her, I would ask her how she spent her day. I could count on her response to be, "I was over at the shopping centre and I picked up a few things" which almost always referred to groceries. As she became more frail, she didn't visit the shopping centre quite as often although she would invariably give me the same response even when the visits decreased in frequency.

The repetitiveness of this activity and recounting it to me seems to have remained with my mother. Several months after she had been admitted to a nursing home facility, I asked her how her day had been. Even though she had not visited the shopping centre or even mentioned it to me for many months, her answer on that particular occasion was, "I was over at the shopping centre and I picked up a few things."

Hats off!

I regularly visited a day program attended by persons with Alzheimer Disease. One day, as usual, I greeted each person by name. I came to a new participant and went to offer my hand. She backed off and glaring at me said, "Do you call that thing on your head a hat? I'm an artist and I know what people should wear and I wouldn't be caught dead with what you have on!"

Eyebrows – beautiful beautiful brown eyes!

My mother always makes sure that her eyebrows are in shape and that her lipstick is on even when she isn't going anywhere. On one occasion as she and I were getting ready to go out, she told me that she needed to finish her eyebrows but was having difficulty with the eyebrow pencil. I went over to check the situation and found her using her regular lead writing pencil. When I explained the problem to my mother, she opened her purse (where she always kept her make-up in a small cosmetic bag), found her real eyebrow pencil and got on with the task at hand without batting an eyelash and as if nothing had happened. Before you knew it, we were on our way out the door – my mother with her beautiful eyebrows!

Wonderful Wonderword

For many years, my mother has been religiously doing the Wonderword, a word puzzle that appears daily in the newspaper. This is one activity she continues to love to do and her ability to complete this has not slackened nor diminished. I always made sure that she had an abundant supply of Wonderword puzzles at hand.

With the onset of Alzheimer Disease, I saw my mother gradually forget how to do so many things. Fortunately, Wonderword was never one of these. Once on a cold winter's day when she was still in her apartment, I remember suggesting that we could each do a Wonderword. I had a good laugh. I decided that I would do mine very slowly to ensure that she completed hers before I did. I needn't have worried because she quickly finished hers long before I was even halfway through mine. When I asked her if she would mind completing mine for me, she was absolutely delighted and did so in no time at all.

If anyone is interested in starting a Wonderword competition, I am certain my mother would do very well as a competitor!

Being alert

Bob, a day program client, was a very pleasant and traditional man. Each day when the driver took him home after the program it was Bob's routine to kiss the staff and the female driver goodbye. One day he kissed the staff and leaned over to kiss the driver who on that day was a man. Bob backed away in surprise and said, "Oh my gosh, man, I almost kissed you!"

A birthday remembered, still

When my husband was diagnosed with Alzheimer Disease, he was advised by his doctor that he could no longer drive his car and that the Ministry of Transportation would be notified. Fortunately, my husband had had cataract surgery and had not driven for the past six months and he told the doctor that he did not drive anymore.

As my birthday approached, the family was talking about it. A few days later, I arrived home to find a birthday card on the kitchen table. It was from my love. I was so surprised. I had not had a card from him for the past few years. I thanked him and asked where he had got the card. He told me he had driven to the store to get it! To this day I don't know how he managed to do this – find the car keys, remember how to drive the car and locate the nearby shopping centre. Something in his memory must have momentarily returned. A few hours later he did not remember doing this. From that day on the car keys were always with me.

Follow the leaders

A friend and I were having supper with my mother at a restaurant. We all ordered tomato juice as a starter. When the tomato juice arrived, I noticed my mother using a spoon for her juice. While my impulsive reaction was to correct her and tell her to drink it, I decided to let it go. In short order, both my friend and I started to drink ours. My mother quickly followed suit abandoning her spoon and drinking the juice as she was accustomed to doing.

Suitcase for a day

I often took my mother to visit family who lived out of town, where more often than not we would stay over for at least one night. With my mother's increasing memory challenges, I would call her before I arrived to remind her what she should pack. Then I would double check when I arrived at her place to make sure nothing important was missing – for example, her medication.

On this occasion, my mother was ready as usual. However, much to my surprise her suitcase was packed and ready to go. I didn't have the heart to tell her that she needn't have packed as we were only going to be gone for the day. So we took the suitcase with us.

Upon returning home that evening, she told me that she had enjoyed the day, wished me a good drive home, and that since she was tired she would unpack in the morning.

I don't think she ever realized that we had been gone only for a day and that she had never used the contents of the suitcase.

A special wave

Like Queen Elizabeth II, my mother, although she probably doesn't realize it, has her own special wave. Whether at her former apartment or now at her residence, I have never known her to forget to wave goodbye to my brother and me from her window or the balcony, regardless of the hour. In time, I discovered that she did this for others to whom she felt close including my friends and a few very special caregivers.

Grandchildren

We take great pleasure in knowing that my mother is somewhat aware of her grandchildren. She has had a strong social influence on them and they visit with her quite often.

"Anna is in New York," she says to us. Or, "Rachel is in Geneva, so far away." Or, "Joshua is studying." When we ask her about her youngest grandchild she replies with a smile, "Jacob is in Montreal and he visits my mother." In fact, her mother died 22 years ago, but we nod and we say, "Yes, indeed, Jacob is in Montreal and studying at McGill. You encouraged us to go to university, remember?" And she smiles and says "Yes."

OUT OF
THE BLUE

NOT ALL THE BEHAVIOURS OF OUR LOVED ones with Alzheimer Disease can be associated with their personalities as we knew them. In the following eight stories, their responses to situations seem to come out of the blue – or perhaps we didn't know our loved ones quite as well as we thought!

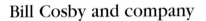

Bill Cosby and company

My mother always loved the actor Bill Cosby. One evening when she and I were watching his show, the phone rang at his house on the television. My mother, who very rarely swore, promptly picked up the phone beside her, expecting Bill to be on the other end. She was surprised to find no one was there. Shrugging her shoulders my mother said "Silly bugger!" then laughed and hung up.

Cookies and then some...

My husband, Ken, a very quiet man, always wanted to help and would shop each day for lunch. He had no trouble finding his way around because he was used to long working days in the bush. I thought he never bought anything but cookies until he went to the hospital and I found dozens of birthday cards that he had hidden in the desk and bureau!

Same time each year

When one of our gentlemen clients of the day program became ill, we needed to call the ambulance. He was unresponsive. When he first awakened his speech was somewhat garbled and he could not answer any questions the paramedics asked. A few minutes later he returned to full alertness. When he was asked his birthdate, he responded with the correct day and month. The paramedic asked, "What year?" Our hilarious client responded, "Every year!" After we all laughed he gave the year as asked.

Jamming the refrigerator

I was yet again cleaning up the contents of my mother's refrigerator and noticed an unusually large number of jars of jam, particularly peach and apricot. My mother had always been fond of jam but up until then had seldom bought anything but strawberry jam. For several months I became the local distributor of jams among my friends as there were at least six to eight jars of jam in her fridge. This pattern stopped as abruptly as it had begun.

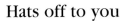

Hats off to you

One winter was exceptional when it came to my mother losing her hats. In a period of less than four months, my mother had seemingly managed to lose four hats. Over the years as my mother's memory was failing, I became better at anticipating certain patterns of losing things. But in the case of the hats I could never find them, no matter how thoroughly I had looked, so I stocked up on several and would always have them with me when I visited her.

So imagine my surprise when well into the spring, I found one of her hats sitting on a chair in the living room. My mother had no idea where it had been nor how it had reappeared. And then even more surprising, in the weeks that followed a second hat reappeared! However, there have still been no sightings of hats three and four.

The story of Ruth

My mother and a small of group of residents had come together for their weekly meeting with an animator. The animator was explaining an upcoming holiday and going over some of the special stories, activities and foods associated with this occasion. She mentioned that often there are stories about women associated with these holidays and she briefly told them the story of Ruth.

During the discussion following the story, my mother asked if there was a story about her (my mother). Since she was always an unassuming person, I was quite surprised to hear her come out with this question. The animator gently replied that there wasn't and that was the end of that. To this day, I do not know if my mother was joking or not!

Cocktails of a different kind

On one visit to my mother's apartment, I noticed a murky looking liquid in her glass and asked her what she was drinking. She said she had mixed a few things together. I asked her, "What few things?" to which she replied, "Coke and milk." Other combinations which I learned about over time were milk and orange juice, and coke and orange juice. What prompted her to mix these concoctions I never did find out. However, for several months, these combinations appeared time and again and from what I could tell, my mother thoroughly enjoyed them.

Beware of moose and deer

When travelling on the highway with my mother at night, I would try to think of an activity to occupy her. One evening we were on a narrow secondary route that was deserted except for two cars a long way ahead of us. I suggested, given the warning signs for moose and deer, that I would concentrate on watching the highway and that she should keep a lookout for moose and deer. She said "Fine," and then added, "If there are some, they probably wouldn't bother us as they likely would hit the cars ahead of us first."

ADAPTING TO LANGUAGE DEFICITS

LANGUAGE IS AN EARLY CASUALTY OF Alzheimer Disease. Yet even as the language deficits become more apparent in our loved ones, so too does their creativity in applying retained learning to communicate the meaning of words. Indeed, as several of the following stories show, these efforts often inadvertently result in puns and witticisms that may cheer us all.

Also of note is their use of early learning methods such as rhymes and repetition to assist in communication.

Language challenges of a different kind

My father had vascular dementia which led to the development of language problems. While this at times was extremely frustrating both for him and for me, there were times when we could only enjoy the humour in what was expressed.

The problems began with simple word substitution. We arranged for a nurse who did foot care to come to the home, and my father thoroughly enjoyed this attention. He was very interested in what she was doing, the implements she was using, and then inquired how many other "victims" she had. At this stage, he was able to join in our enjoyment of what he had said.

My father would also insert whatever caught his attention into a comment even though it had no relevance to the situation. On one occasion we were driving together from Toronto to Ottawa. At that time, Dad had developed a keen interest (to the point of it being a fixation) in license plates. My husband had left earlier than we had to make the same trip. In talking about whether or not my husband might already be in Ottawa, my father figured he certainly would be because, "He left before they started putting numbers on license plates."

A "punny" presence

My brother-in-law, Hamilton, had always been a great punster. As Alzheimer Disease advanced he lost some of his quickness. Then when we were all at a birthday party just a month before he died, this happened: after lunch my sister said, "Time for presents," and Ham immediately responded, "You mean my presence isn't enough?"

Leaf it there!

One of the day program staff was out for a walk with a client. The staff member looked down and said, "I have a leaf caught on my shoe." The client replied, "Why don't you leaf it there?"

Couplets – the poetic version

One of the numerous habits that my mother developed along her Alzheimer journey was the repetition of familiar phrases. In particular, she started to frequently use the expressions, "How now, brown cow," and, "See you later, alligator." I am uncertain what sparked this as I have no recollection of her using those expressions frequently before. On one occasion when she initiated those phrases with me, shortly afterwards I replied, "In a while, crocodile." My mother quickly incorporated this into her script. While she may have trouble learning many other things, my mother has had no trouble making that addition to her repertoire. So if you are ever in her company for a while, you are likely to hear, "How now, brown cow / See you later, alligator / In a while, crocodile." These playful repetitions appear to give her much pleasure.

***

More creative responses

As my father's language skills deteriorated, there were times when he was totally unintelligible. What I found completely mystifying was that one minute he could make no sense yet the next be completely articulate. On one occasion when he was communicating with only a jumble of sounds, I remarked, "That sounds very complicated, Dad." Absolutely clearly, my father, an electrical engineer by profession, replied, "Oh, I've just reduced it all to mathematical formula," which he probably had.

Another problem for my father was identifying where he was, and the objects around him. The location of the stairs was a major puzzle to him, but to him the problem was not that he couldn't find the stairs. Rather his standard comment was, "You've moved the stairs again," which I somehow managed to do every day.

Object confusion led to his trying to do things with inappropriate objects, such as the time he tried to turn on the TV with a table napkin. My daughter was amused when I remarked to my father that as that one didn't work, we better try another one (the actual TV remote control), and thus resolved the situation.

Television connections

Although my father had been an electrical engineer and a problem solver all his life, managing the television remote control became a problem. One day he wasn't able to turn off the television. I showed him how, but he said he had already tried, and asked me to try. When it turned off, Dad exclaimed, "Well I'll be darned. How did you do that?"

My father also began to have hallucinations, and often felt other people were around, which led to some humorous moments. The TV at times compounded this problem for him. One evening when he was ready to go to bed, he informed me that he had given the television remote control to Jean Chrétien!

A favour

I was walking down the hall with a day program client when I linked my arm with his. He looked and said, "My wife and your husband won't like this." I replied, "I don't have a husband." He quipped back, "You did some guy a favour and he doesn't even know it."

The curious incident with the dog

One day I visited a woman who was very unhappy about having strangers in her house. When a small dog entered the room, I, yet another stranger, brightly said, "What a cute dog. What's its name?" She looked at me pityingly, and scornfully said, "It's a DOG."

Substituting this for that

As my mother's disease progressed, she had difficulty finding words, a problem that she'd never had in the past. She developed a wonderful ability to communicate with phrases that substituted for the words that no longer came readily to her.

For example, as usual I had mailed her a birthday card. When I called her in the evening to wish her a happy birthday, she was appreciative of the phone call and thanked me. The words "birthday card" failed her and so in their stead, she thanked me for what I had sent her in the mail.

Another evening when I called her, I asked her what she was doing. She told me that she was watching TV and (having difficulty finding the word for "bed") said that she was, "Sitting on the place where I lie down at night," and playing cards.

On yet another occasion when I called her, the phone rang about four times before she picked it up. When she did, she said, "Hello?" and then apologized for being "late" to answer the phone.

She seems very at ease and not the least upset when she is using these substitutions. Perhaps she is not even aware that she is doing it.

More puns

A day program staff member was sitting beside one of the gentlemen clients. She looked down at her bare feet in her shoes and commented, "I have my bare feet today." The client responded, "The poor bear!"

And more puns

One day I was passing around cheese and crackers to the clients of the day program and asked Joe, "Would you like a piece of cheese?" He replied, "No." I asked, "Do you want a cracker?" He again replied, "No." About half an hour later he said to me, "I don't hit women, you know." I said, "Why Joe I never said you did." He replied, "Yes, you did. You asked me if I wanna crack 'er!"

The marvels of travel

My mother has always enjoyed going for a drive in the car. With her memory challenges, her ability to engage in conversation is very limited. However, she continues to take great pride in repeating over and over again how beautiful the flowers are, how terrible the potholes are in the summer, how lovely the lights are at Christmas time, and she is relentless in announcing the upcoming green, yellow or red traffic lights throughout the year.

Bedtime

About two and a half years ago, out of the clear blue, my mother started to routinely end our evening telephone conversation with,

> Good night, sleep tight
> Don't let the bugs bite
> If they do, take a shoe,
> And beat them 'til they're black and blue.

When we were kids, my parents would often recite the first part of this verse: "Good night, sleep tight / Don't let the bugs bite."

I don't know what prompted the return to this rhyme nor do I know where my mother picked up the ending. However, hearing her recite it brings a warm feeling to me, especially because my mother seems to be so proud each time she says this.

Pasta analogy

One day a woman I know was trying to tell me how she felt and she said, "My head is like spaghetti. I try to pull out what I want to say and it goes back in."

ADAPTING TO THE ENVIRONMENT

OUR LOVED ONES STRUGGLE TO MAKE sense out of their familiar environments. Their efforts meet with varying degrees of success as the following two accounts show.

Output is only as good as the input and the right input device!

My mother has a few favourite television programs including *Jeopardy* and *Wheel of Fortune*. She always remembers to watch them and still needs no prompting to do so. She also enjoys special shows such as musicals and skating competitions. As it became increasingly more difficult for her to use the television program guide to determine when these shows were on, I tried to do it for her long distance.

When I spotted something in the program guide that I thought would be of interest to her, I would call her and instruct her in which numbers to press on her television remote control. This arrangement worked exceptionally well until about a year ago.

I called my mother to tell her about a specific program and gave her the information as in the past. The next thing I heard was the noise of her pressing buttons and I concluded that she was pressing the respective buttons on her telephone pad. I kept trying to get her attention by yelling into the mouthpiece of my phone. All I could hear was her saying, "It's not working and I don't understand why!"

It occurred to me that if I didn't get her attention soon, at least one of our phones would be out of commission for a while. Fortunately my mother soon returned the phone to her ear. I discontinued this practice and replaced it with a modified (but more foolproof) approach. So far, so good.

Hide and Seek – my mother's version

A friend and I were having tea and cake at my mother's apartment one day. I inquired about some correspondence that my mother was to have received and passed on to me. My mother acknowledged receiving it and proceeded to look in all the usual places – her bedroom dresser, the credenza in the living room, the hall table at the entrance of her apartment, and so on. She returned to the dining room table without any document.

Almost immediately after sitting down, she had a special look in her eye, and said she knew where it was. She went to the kitchen and sure enough returned with the document in her hands. When we asked her where she had found it, she told us, "It was in the oven." Perfectly sensible, since by this time the fuses had been removed and my mother had long since stopped using her oven!

ENJOYING THE MOMENT

THE KEEN PLEASURE THAT PERSONS WITH Alzheimer Disease continue to derive from their long-established sources of enjoyment is encouraging and comforting to family and friends.

Photo delight

My mother always has enjoyed looking at family photographs taken over the years. Whenever I visited with her, we would go over the photos. It was interesting to see that she was still able to recognize those persons familiar to her. Although this ability has continued to decline over the years, there are still a select few persons whom she can identify.

Recently, I brought a set of photos to my mother. As always she was able to identify most of the individuals. However, the difference this time around was that once we had looked at all the photos, she started over (and over) completely forgetting that she had just looked at all of them. Even though she went over the photos several times, she continued to take delight in looking at them each time as if seeing them for the first time.

Forever sharing

My mother will often say that she isn't hungry although in reality she eats well. A healthy breakfast, a snack, a cup of coffee – she loves her coffee. Sometimes I go with her for lunch in the residence. It is a substantial meal: stewed meat, potatoes, vegetables, soup. She says she isn't hungry but with time and patience, as I cut the food on her plate and remind her what is on her fork, she eats her way through the meal. If I reach with my fork to taste something from her plate, she is particularly pleased. She enjoys sharing with me, just as she always did when I was her younger child.

Four leaf clover

My sister loved to look for four-leaf clovers. On one occasion she was searching for them diligently on her front lawn when suddenly she stopped to look up and shout with delight, "See those birds. The same ones come every day." Then with joy she picked a four leafer out of the lawn and presented it to me, saying, "Especially for you."

The pleasure of the visit

My wife and I visit my mother in Montreal regularly and because we travel in from Ottawa these visits usually are quite long. I sit with her, tell her about recent news and doings, and walk with her down the hall or, if the weather is good, we walk outdoors. My wife usually joins us and we will talk a while and often go for lunch together in the dining room of the residence.

One of these visits was particularly warm, my mother happily responding to our activities. A day later my brother went to see her and asked her about our visit. "Oh," she replied, "I haven't spoken to him in a long time."

My first reaction on hearing about this was deep disappointment, even some anger. I had spent three hours with my mother and, one day later, she had no memory of it. Later, as I thought about this more carefully, I realized that the purpose of my visits does not lie in giving my mother pleasant memories. The purpose is achieved in the moment itself and any future memories will be mine, not hers.

She smiles with delight when I come into her room. We hold hands. She nods and says a few words in reply to my direct questions. She wishes me a fond goodbye when I leave. It is the pleasure of these moments that count for her.

Their impact on us

One way to look after our own emotional needs is with humour. It can work wonders by helping us to cope with care-giving demands. However, trying to find some humour in situations that might not be funny isn't always easy. It can be distressing for a caregiver to suddenly have to cope with a loved one's anger, hallucinations or inappropriate behaviour in public. Some days it may be possible to laugh, others it may not.

Our storytellers demonstrate that it is possible to find humour in day-to-day situations. As you wind your way through sharing their experiences, you too might be able to find some support and humour in your contact with a person close to you with Alzheimer Disease. From the title of each anecdote, we hope you will take heart and realize that there is usually some humour to be found.

Expect the unexpected – always a first time!

For a few years as my mother's condition began to deteriorate, I travelled to Montreal to accompany her on key medical appointments.

On this particular occasion, I arranged to pick her up early in the afternoon for her mid-afternoon appointment. As I pulled up in front of her apartment building, I realized that my mother had just walked past my car with a very focused expression on her face.

When I called out to her, she expressed both surprise and delight in seeing me. She told me that she was on her way to the shopping centre to pick up a few things. This was a common outing and almost the only one she could manage on her own. She then asked me if I would like to join her. I said, "Yes", and we headed off to her medical appointment first.

I was so very relieved that our paths had crossed! I know how concerned I would have been had I arrived to find her apartment empty. Variations of this situation subsequently arose, fortunately without any untoward outcomes.

———

False optimism

As it became more and more apparent that my mother's condition was deteriorating, I asked her to seriously consider an alternative living arrangement to her own apartment. I explained that this would give me peace of mind since I was becoming concerned about her safety.

To placate me (or so it seemed to me), she agreed and went with me to visit a seniors' residence in her neighbourhood. After this visit it became obvious that I should forget any ideas that I had about an alternate living arrangement.

At the first and only place we visited, the administrator and nurse in charge gave us a full tour through several units and the common rooms. It turned out that my mother already knew several residents. We saw a few of them as we toured the building and she chatted very animatedly with them.

She showed considerable interest during the visit and commented favourably on aspects such as the cleanliness and the size of the apartments.

Enroute back to her apartment, I asked my mother what she thought. Without any hesitation, she told me that the place was very nice but that she was fine in her own apartment. She had no intention of moving and there was no need for her to move. Discussion closed!

My son – her grandson – the banker

My mother struggled with memory loss for several years. As she deteriorated the family continued to provide assistance, trying to leave her with as much independence as possible.

On one particular visit to Ottawa from Western Canada, my son, who lived in the same city as she did, had agreed to accompany his grandmother to Ottawa for Christmas because she could no longer travel on her own.

During the flight, my mother started fidgeting with what seemed to be lots of paper in her purse. She casually leaned over and asked my son if he would help her organize her papers. My son gladly complied, and she turned them over to him. Much to his surprise the "papers" were twenty-dollar bills totalling approximately $2,000. Although we were monitoring my mother's affairs, we hadn't yet taken the drastic step of limiting the amount she could withdraw from her bank accounts since she still withdrew very small sums.

Shortly after their arrival in Ottawa, we deposited the money back into Mom's account and then took precautionary measures to avoid similar surprises in the future.

Forever caring

Parting from each other is hard for wives and husbands. For some it is unbearable. One woman, who was unable to accept her husband's decline at home, was no happier when he became a resident in a good nursing home. He spent his days there holding hands with an equally sad woman. His wife was so distraught that she complained to the nurses that the woman was stealing her husband and they had to get rid of her.

Factual phone calls

I often phone my mother in the morning before starting my work. The conversation we have is really one-way, as my mother rarely talks in a complete sentence or expresses a full thought. So I tell her about my children, my wife, and our friends. I'll remind her several times that I am in Ottawa, telling her about our weather and asking her about the weather in Montreal. "I am not in Montreal," she often replies, "I am in Côte St. Luc" (a suburb of Montreal).

During other phone calls she will ask me about my wife, remembering her name without hesitation. When our call is ending, she will say, "I like to hear your voice. Are you coming to see me?"

Family photos

On one of my recent visits with Mom, we were sitting on her bed in the nursing home, going through an old family photo album as we did each time I visited her. When we got to a picture of me as a little girl, Mom turned to me with quite a serious face and asked, "What ever happened to her?" I answered, "She grew up and is sitting beside you right now!" We both burst out laughing at the same time at our funny joke. This is a story from a daughter now age fifty-five.

Sweet tooth

As far back as I can remember my mother has had a sweet tooth, and still does. From my observation, as her memory problems increase, so does her obsession with sweets.

One afternoon my mother and I were celebrating

my brother's birthday with him. We had brought a birthday cake with us for the occasion. My mother, my brother and I each had a very respectable piece of birthday cake. Suddenly, I detected some mischief in my mother's eyes and noticed her cunning attempt to cut herself another piece of cake without being noticed. I didn't say anything so she had her cake and ate it, too...two times!

After leaving my brother and the remainder of the cake, I told my mother that I wanted a cup of coffee so we stopped at a nearby coffee shop before returning to her apartment. I asked my mother if she would like something to drink. She said "No" but quickly informed me that she would have a piece of cake. She had noticed the sweet selection on her way in. I tried to discourage her but to no avail. So I resorted to some cunning myself. Upon ordering the sweet for her, I told the server to cut a very small piece from what I had ordered and that's what I gave my mother. She thoroughly enjoyed it!

As the butter melts

While my mother's hoarding patterns were not extreme, she did develop some over time. Whenever we go out to eat, she loves to put in her purse the small containers of butter, packets of sugar, and the little containers of milk and cream used for coffee and tea. I have not been very successful in discouraging this behaviour, though it certainly isn't for lack of gently trying to do so. On numerous occasions this has led to soiled purses after the butter melted and the milk turned sour. As a result, when I am fast enough, I will try my hardest to remove from her sight all these types of items.

I will never forget an occasion when I hadn't acted quickly enough. We were drinking our coffee and two or three containers of milk remained on the table in a small dish. She discreetly and gradually moved the dish closer to her. Then when she thought it was close enough, she distracted me (or so she thought) by pointing at something for me to see as she quietly put the loot in her purse.

That evening after we returned from the restaurant, I waited for the appropriate opportunity, then removed the loot from her purse before yet another one was soiled, without letting on that she had been caught in the act. From her perspective, it was mission successful and remained that way.

A residence is a residence is a hotel?

My mother had resisted moving for a long time. I had tried without success to convince her to move to a seniors' residence even before her memory deteriorated significantly. After several years of decline, it became clear that it was no longer possible for her to remain in her apartment and that the time had come to apply for admission to a nursing home. During the lengthy wait for admission, my mother had a crisis situation that required immediate attention. An interim placement was found since there was no room in the preferred residence. I moved my mother into what was to become her new home. This move occurred against her will and with much shedding of tears on my part, despite the tremendous support of my friends.

The first few weeks were very difficult for me. Whenever I spoke to my mother she routinely asked me when I would be taking her back to her apartment. On one visit, I found that she had packed all her clothes anticipating that I would be taking her back there. All the while she was settling in quite nicely, even though she was still asking when she would be returning to her apartment. Gradually this behaviour diminished. I even found myself laughing. On one occasion when I told her I would be coming into town to visit her, she asked me if I would be meeting her at her apartment or at her hotel.

Never say never

For over a year I had been trying to convince my mother to move, and had completed the application for a long-term care setting. I had expressed both my and her doctor's concerns about her safety and I worried a lot about her because I lived so far away. I made absolutely no progress in convincing my mother. I realized that I would likely have to wait for a crisis before any move would occur. My mother had been on a waiting list for placement in a long-term care facility. Since she had resisted any voluntary move to a seniors' residence, I was certain that she would react very negatively to the move when it happened.

When the time did arrive, I dreaded the day of the move but with the strong support of my friends, I got through it and so did my mother. The first couple of days and even weeks were difficult, probably more so for me than for my mother. She adjusted incredibly well and quickly to her new environment – she made new friends, loved the food (in fact, put on too much weight in the first eight months), and participated in exercise sessions and arts and crafts.

Never would I have imagined that the outcome would be so wonderful!

Caring connections

Everyone benefits when the community is more aware of what it means to live with Alzheimer Disease. As our stories illustrate, the quality of life for everyone is improved when the next-door neighbour, the policeman or the family doctor act on this awareness.

Our storytellers will tell you how the understanding and cooperation of our community is invaluable to people with Alzheimer Disease and their families. As we watch the disease take its toll, the connections to the community that we have, and that our loved ones have, bring enjoyment and grateful relief to all of us.

Guardian accountant

After my dad passed away many years ago, my mother took on the annual task of visiting the accountant. She continued to do this even after she developed problems with her memory. At one point my mother's accountant moved his office to a different area of the city. She was familiar with this area but had not been there in a long time. The change in office location occurred at a time when my mother was experiencing great difficulty in learning to navigate a new route. She could manage to get to a few places she had been going to for many years (her beauty parlour, her seniors' group, and the local shopping mall) but it had become virtually impossible for her to learn a new route or to go to once familiar, but rarely visited places.

My mother's accountant told me the following story soon after it happened. My mother got lost on her way to his new office. Fortunately she had the awareness to call him from a pay phone close by. Her darling accountant insisted that she stay where she was and arranged for her to be picked up and safely transported to his office. She remained there until he was able to drive her home. Apparently, my mother seemed totally unconcerned about getting lost. Her accountant, whom she has known for decades, could not have been kinder or more compassionate.

Yet another Alzheimer moment

Every spring it's time to open the swimming pool for the summer season. One year, the pool company had been booked and all the equipment placed in the back garden ready for them. Just before the pool company was due to arrive, I told my husband that I was going into the back garden and that when the pool company staff arrived he should tell them to go to the back garden. He said "Okay".

The pool service people arrived moments later, rang the front door bell and were met by my anxious husband who yelled, "Go away, not today!" and then slammed the door.

Fortunately they had the sense to check out the back garden. They still tell this story years later.

Hearing restored

Several years ago when my mother was still living on her own in an apartment, I received a call from her dear neighbours to alert me that my mother had suddenly lost her hearing in both ears. They told me that she had been to the hospital emergency department, and that an appointment was booked for the following morning with an ear, nose and throat specialist. A taxi driver was to pick her up to take her to her appointment.

However, my mother completely forgot about the appointment, and of course, when the taxi driver rang her bell and then knocked on her door, she did not hear him. When I called her neighbours at noon to find out the results from the doctor's visit, they (having a key to my mother's apartment), checked in on her and found out what had happened.

When I learned that she had missed her appointment, I decided to drive immediately to Montreal (it was Friday afternoon) and see if I could address this problem before the weekend. It was all very hectic but with the help of my mother's neighbours we had an appointment with their own ear, nose and throat specialist in the late afternoon.

After my mother had been only a few moments in the doctor's office, he came into the waiting area and asked me to join them. He showed me the cause of her deafness – wads of cotton and Kleenex which my mother had put into her ears! We never did know why she did this and of course she had no recollection of doing so.

For the next several months, I put signs in her bathroom and bedroom stating, "Please do not put anything into your ears!" As well, the caregivers who were visiting her – by now, seven days a week – would constantly check to see if anything had been inserted in her ears. Occasionally there was some cotton or Kleenex there that was easily removed. Eventually this habit stopped completely.

The "odd couple"

One of our most wonderful caregivers was Frances, a Hungarian lady. She and my mother became known as "the odd couple." My mother was the thin, prim and proper, Anglo-Saxon Protestant, and Frances was the heavy, outspoken salt-of-the-earth, Eastern European Catholic. The two of them would often be seen, walking hand-in-hand, chatting away – seemingly deep in conversation. The situation was both comical and remarkable since many people had trouble understanding Frances' accent and peculiar sense of humour, and also had trouble understanding my mother whose communications skills had all but disappeared. Yet somehow they understood each other perfectly well.

Social network to the rescue

For many years my mother belonged to a social club for seniors and attended all the activities. The dates for events and meetings of this club were sacred to her. Everyone who knew her knew that Wednesdays were for her social club. She loved the movies, the bingo, the musical groups that visited and the special guest speakers. She also participated regularly in the various outings and occasional trips that were organized.

One such event was the trip to the casino which was a full-day event. Members were to be picked up by bus at designated locations mid-morning and returned by late afternoon. My mother was already having substantial memory problems by this time.

Upon arrival at the casino, members were given the option either to leave their coats on the bus or to take them into the casino and check them. My mother opted to check her coat.

When the group was all aboard the bus and ready to return home that afternoon, the person sitting beside my mother noticed that my mother didn't have her coat. This woman asked the bus driver to delay the departure and asked my mother if she had checked her coat. My mother couldn't remember. She then asked my mother if she could check her purse for a coat check stub. She found the stub and quickly went to get the coat.

You might wonder how I came to know that this had happened. Certainly my mother had no recollection of it. A few weeks after the trip to the casino, I was visiting my mother, and we were at the local mall. A woman with a gentle smile approached us, said hello to my mother and asked if I was her daughter. My mother couldn't remember the person's name. However, she certainly recognized her and told her that I was her daughter. This delightful lady was the person who had sat beside my mother on that bus to the casino. She jokingly said, "I see your mother is wearing her coat. It's a good thing we were able to retrieve it since the weather has been so cold these past few weeks." I of course then asked about what had happened and she related the story about the coat to me.

Quite soon after this, it became necessary for me to arrange for a companion to accompany my mother on these outings. Despite this, she continued to enjoy the outings and to the best of my knowledge, the members of the club continued to be very kind to her.

Good habits and the kindness of strangers

My grandfather, a businessman in Quebec City, retired in his early sixties as a result of what everyone then called senility. Still physically robust and by nature gregarious, every day he set out on a walk of several hours' duration around the city. For many years, although he gradually could no longer recognize his grandchildren and then his children, he was able to find his way back from these walks to the house where he had lived with my grandmother for fifty years. However, as he approached eighty, he began to get lost. A series of people – complete strangers to my grandmother – then began bringing him home. These were people accustomed to seeing and speaking with him on his route over the years!

Interestingly, even at this time, his language abilities (or disabilities) were no worse in French than in English, although French was not his mother tongue.

Man's best friend

We live a block away from the Rideau River, close to downtown. One evening I went out for an early evening walk with the dog, leaving my husband, who was in the early stages of Alzheimer Disease, at home. When it began to get dark, I phoned him on my cell phone to tell him I was a few blocks away on a neighbouring street.

When I rounded the corner to our street, I saw a police car outside the house and my husband in conversation with an officer.

As I approached them, the officer quipped, "Your husband thought he'd never see the dog again!"

Apparently my husband had caught sight of the patrol car when he was looking up and down the street for me, having forgotten that I had just called with a reassuring message. He explained to the officer that I had been gone a long time and that he was concerned because it was getting dark. The officer then took a drive along the National Capital Commission parkland and riverbank looking for a woman and a dog!

Beauty parlour on wheels

My mother takes pride in her hair and for many years went to the same beauty parlour, which was within walking distance of her apartment. Even when her condition deteriorated, I arranged for the caregivers to escort her to and from her beauty parlour appointments.

So it was quite natural that when she moved into a nursing home, I made arrangements with the home for her to have her hair done every week. Within a few weeks, I learned that the home had tried to take care of this, but my mother refused to allow the person to do her hair. She insisted that she had always gone to her own beauty parlour every week and would continue to do so.

Upon learning of this situation, I contacted her former beauty parlour and asked if the person who had done her hair could go to her new home and continue her hair care. When they said they would organize this, I was delighted – and so was my mother, it turned out. When her former hairdresser arrived to take care of her hair, my mother was very receptive. This arrangement continues and I am very grateful to the beauty parlour for being so flexible in accommodating this request.

Skin care – a new product

Over the years, my mother developed numerous non-malignant blotches on her face. This troubled her because she did not like the way it looked. When she asked her physician for suggestions, he recommended a particular over-the-counter face cream.

She used this product quite successfully for several years. On one of my visits home, my mother told me that she had run out of this cream and wanted to buy some more.

So we visited her drugstore to do just that. When she couldn't find the product, I offered to help her look for it, but I couldn't find it either. I then asked a salesperson for assistance. She immediately recognized my mother and very politely explained to me that my mother had already been in on several occasions looking for this product and had been advised that the product had been discontinued. She had also tried to explain to my mother that there were similar products which she could use in its place but to no avail.

I thanked her for her patience and then discreetly went ahead and bought one of the other products the salesperson had recommended.

When we returned to her apartment, I suggested to my mother that she try the other cream. She did and although it took a little while, she gradually became accustomed to the different packaging and name and was soon using the new product in place of her previous one.

Reality check

Almost from her first day in the residence, my mother enjoyed participating in the various activities including bingo, exercises, crafts, and singalongs.

She had been in the residence for close to nine months when a small group of seven or eight residents were brought together by an animator one afternoon to begin a general learning and exploring knowledge group. My mother expressed an interest in attending and as I was visiting, I was invited to sit in with the group for its first meeting.

The animator asked the participants to introduce themselves and to say a few words about themselves – for example, where they were born, how old they were (if they felt comfortable with that), and what languages they spoke. When my mother's turn came, her answer was similar to what others had said, with one curious exception: she concluded by giving her previous address and stating that's where she lived!

Fortunately, no one pointed out to her that she now lived at a new address.

The family connection

My husband was placed in a long-term care facility near the end of his Alzheimer journey. It was my birthday, the first without him there to share it with me after many wonderful years together.

My children knew this would be a difficult day for me and invited me to celebrate my birthday with them. On the table was a vase of red roses with a card saying the roses were from my husband with his love.

There was a birthday card for me with the following poem that had been written by my daughter. This poem reflected my children's perception of the relationship between my husband and me throughout our marriage and parenthood.

Their love and support helped me through the most difficult period of my life.

The poem read:

For my darling Joan on her birthday –

If I could…
I would shower you with roses
Throw emeralds at your feet
Submerge you in diamonds
Announce my love to the world

If I could…
I would embrace you tightly
To affirm that
You
Are the centre of my being
My touchstone
My one and only true
Love

If I could…
I would shout this to the heavens
Stop strangers in the street
Have them marvel at the beauty of your soul
As I do

But I cannot

Yet all this is truth
Even though I may forget

So you
My darling Joan
Must remember this always
For me.

Conclusion

W e hope that these lighter reflections on a very difficult journey have managed to bring a smile to your face. If you have had similar light-hearted experiences with your loved ones with Alzheimer Disease, please consider jotting down your own stories and sharing them with others.

Our community will need increasingly more resources to care for persons with Alzheimer Disease in the coming years. We encourage you to support the Alzheimer Society of Ottawa by recommending this book to your family and friends, and by supporting other local fundraising initiatives.